HOW TO IMPROVE AT TENNIS

All the information you need to know to get on top of your game!

More than just instructional guides, the **HOW TO IMPROVE AT...** series gives you everything you need to achieve your goals—tips on technique, step-by-step demonstrations, nutritional advice, and the secrets of successful pro athletes. Excellent visual instructions and expert advice combine to act as your own personal trainer. These books aim to give you the know-how and confidence to improve your performance.

Studies have shown that an active approach to life makes you feel happier and less stressed. The easiest way to start is by taking up a new sport or improving your skills in an existing one. You simply have to choose an activity that enthuses you.

HOW TO IMPROVE AT TENNIS does not promise instant success. It simply gives you the tools to become the best at whatever you choose to do.

Every care has been taken to ensure that these instructions are safe to follow, but in the event of injury Crabtree Publishing shall not be liable for any injuries or damages.

By Jim Drewett

 Crabtree Publishing Company
www.crabtreebooks.com

Cover: Tennis star Roger Federer
Special thank you to: Elizabeth Wiggans
Photography: Roddy Paine Photographic Studios
Illustrations: John Alston

Photo credits: Empics: p. 45 bottom, p. 46 right, p. 47 top, and bottom right; Icon SMI/Julien Crosnier/DPPI: front cover; © Shutterstock.com: Paul Cowan: p. 46 left; Vasily Smirnov: p. 47 bottom left.

Library and Archives Canada Cataloguing in Publication

Drewett, Jim
How to improve at tennis / Jim Drewett.

(How to improve at...)
Includes index.
ISBN 978-0-7787-3571-7 (bound).--ISBN 978-0-7787-3593-9 (pbk.)

1. Tennis--Training--Juvenile literature. I. Title. II. Series.

GV996.5.D74 2007   j796.342   C2007-904702-5

Library of Congress Cataloging-in-Publication Data

Drewett, Jim.
How to improve at tennis / Jim Drewett.
p. cm. -- (How to improve at--)
Includes index.
ISBN-13: 978-0-7787-3571-7 (rlb)
ISBN-10: 0-7787-3571-0 (rlb)
ISBN-13: 978-0-7787-3593-9 (pb)
ISBN-10: 0-7787-3593-1 (pb)
1. Tennis for children--Training--Juvenile literature. I. Title. II. Series.

GV1001.4.C45D74 2008
796.342083--dc22   2007030345

Crabtree Publishing Company
www.crabtreebooks.com   1-800-387-7650

Published in Canada
Crabtree Publishing
616 Welland Ave.
St. Catharines, Ontario
L2M 5V6

Published in the United States
Crabtree Publishing
PMB16A
350 Fifth Ave., Suite 3308
New York, NY 10118

Published by CRABTREE PUBLISHING COMPANY
Copyright © **2008**

CONTENTS

INTRODUCTION

*T*ennis is a game of speed and agility that is exciting and fun to play. The major tournaments, such as Wimbledon and the U.S., Australian, and French Open, are watched by millions and many high-ranking players have become household names. Mastering tennis skills takes practice, but the rewards are worth it.

GUIDE TO SYMBOLS & ARROWS

To help you understand movement and direction, we have used the following:

- • • ▶ **1st strike of the ball**
- ⟶ **2nd strike**
- ⟶ **3rd and subsequent strikes**
- • • • • **Practice cones**

The red arrow indicates movement of the body and racket

The yellow arrow indicates movement of the ball

The inset diagrams illustrate the contact point of the ball and racket

All of the instructions in this book are intended for right handed players. Left handed players should simply reverse the instructions.

THE COURT

When you are learning tennis, you can practice your skills by hitting a ball against a wall or playing rallies with friends where there is a flat, hard surface. To play a proper match, however, you need a tennis court.

WHITE LINES

The markings on a tennis court are always white and indicate the borders of the court and service courts. The ball is counted as "in" if any part of the ball lands on the line, and 'out' if it lands on the other side of it.

THE BASELINE

The baseline marks each end of the court. The ball must land on or inside this lin when hit from the opposite side of the net. Players must also have both feet behind this line when serving. It is 36 feet (10.97 m) long.

BASELINE CENTER MARK

This marks the center of the baseline. Players serving on the right of this mark—looking up the court—must serve diagonally into the left-hand service box on the other side of the net, and vice versa. To start serving in a game, you must serve from the right-hand side of the court.

SINGLES SIDELINES

The single sidelines mark the outer edges of the court for a singles match. They are 39 feet (11.89 m) long on either side of the net and 78 feet (23.77 m) long down the length of the whole court.

DOUBLES SIDELINES

These lines indicate the edges of the court for a doubles match. The double sidelines are 4.5 feet (1.37 m) wide of the single sidelines. Together, these sets of lines are known as the "tramlines".

CENTER SERVICE LINE

The center service line divides the area between the net and the service line into two service boxes.

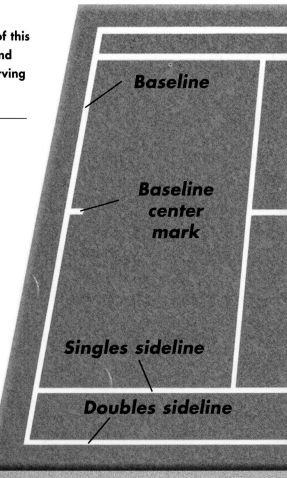

Baseline

Baseline center mark

Singles sideline

Doubles sideline

A tennis court can be on a variety of surfaces. The three main surfaces are hardcourt (concrete), grass, and clay, but you can also play on polished wood or even types of plastic. Rough surfaces, such as clay, slow the ball down but make it bounce higher. Fast surfaces, such as grass, make the ball skid and stay low as it bounces.

THE NET

The net is suspended from two posts that are 3.5 feet (1.07 m) high and stand 3 feet (0.91 m) outside the court. The center of the net measures 3 feet (0.91 m) high.

The service line is at a 90 degree angle to the center service line. A ball landing between this line, the center service line, the single sideline and the net is counted as "in".

The service box is the legal area into which the ball is served. There are two service boxes on each side of the court, measuring 21 feet (6.4 m) in length and 13.5 feet (4.12 m) in width. The server stands to one side of the baseline center mark and serves the ball into the service box diagonally opposite. Service alternates between the right and left sides of the court after each point is scored.

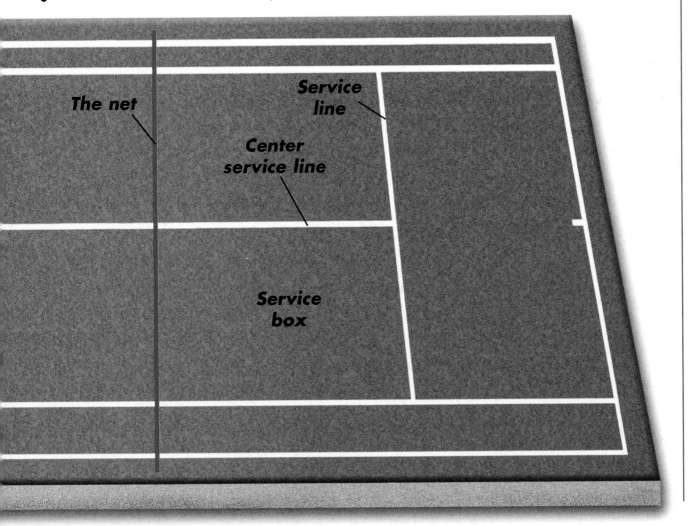

The net

Service line

Center service line

Service box

EQUIPMENT

New and cheaper materials mean that there is a larger range of tennis equipment on the market than there used to be. Be sure to choose durable items that feel comfortable to wear and are easy to use.

SHIRT

A tennis shirt must be loose enough to be comfortable, but not too big that it gets in the way. Get a shirt made of a soft, natural material (like cotton) to absorb sweat. Many shirts also feature small air holes to give ventilation while you play.

SHORTS

Tennis shorts should be loose and comfortable, but strong enough to handle a fall. Pockets are useful for storing a second ball when serving.

SOCKS

The best socks are made of cotton to absorb sweat, and are thick on the sole and heel areas to prevent blisters.

BALLS

Tennis balls are 2.5–2.625 inches (6.35–6.67 cm) in diameter. They are made of two sections of rubber that are fused together and then covered in a tough, fibrous combination of wool and synthetic material. The most common color for tennis balls is fluorescent yellow.

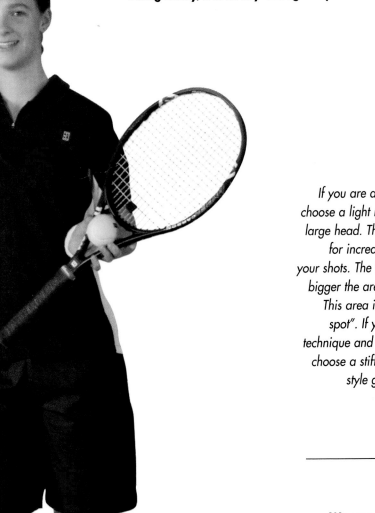

There are many kinds of rackets made to suit different standards and styles of play. To choose the right racket, find one that feels comfortable. It should be light enough to swing easily, but heavy enough to put some power into your shots.

head — _racket face_

If you are a beginner, choose a light racket with a large head. This will be good for increasing the power of your shots. The larger the head, the bigger the area for hitting the ball. This area is known as the "sweet spot". If you already have good technique and can hit powerful shots, choose a stiffer, heavier racket. This style gives you more control.

throat

handle

butt

Women generally wear shorts, but tennis skirts and dresses are also available. They should be short enough to allow complete freedom of movement. Stretch fabrics are good, as they are light and strong.

It is extremely important to have the right shoes. They must be light and comfortable. The leather and synthetic upper part provides flexibility as well as support for the foot, ankle and toes. Non-marking soles are needed to play on most tennis courts. Tennis shoes are different from the cross trainers or running shoes. Their rubber soles are designed to give maximum grip on the court.

BODY POSITION

One of the most important lessons to learn in tennis is how to position your body to play a shot. Good footwork helps you prepare for your shot as soon as the ball is played to you. Get into position early so that you can react to your opponent's shot. If you wait until the ball is right in front of you, it will be too late.

READY POSITION

The ready position is the stance taken between shots. It gives great flexibility and balance to return a shot.

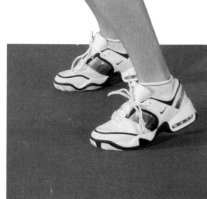

SPLIT–STEP POSITION

The split–step is a small bounce that you make just before moving to the ball. The timing of it is important. Try to make your bounce just before your opponent strikes the ball. This makes you alert and ready to move in any direction.

STEP 1 After the split step, turn in the direction of the ball coming toward you. Take the racket back and move to the ball, in this case with a forehand stroke (see pages 16–17).

STEP 2

As you approach the ball, judge your distance from it so you can hit it comfortably. This is called the "contact point", where the ball is in front of your body, but not too close. Hit the ball in the direction that you want it to go.

STEP 3

Get back into the ready position to prepare for the next shot.

BEING A GOOD TENNIS PLAYER IS ABOUT MASTERING SEVERAL SKILLS AT ONCE. YOU NEED TO:

- be alert to anticipate the movement of the ball and reach it in time for a good return.
- always focus on the ball.
- stay balanced with a low center of gravity.
- use the split step to reach the ball quickly.
- judge the angle of your racket and the direction of the ball in order to play the best return shot.
- adjust the power of your swing to return the best shot.

GRIPS

The way that you hold your tennis racket is called your "grip". There are a variety of correct grips, but some are better than others in certain situations or when playing a particular shot. The most important things are that your grip feels comfortable and that you are able to hit the ball cleanly.

RIGHT-HANDED OR LEFT-HANDED?

All of the grips shown here are for right-handed players. If you are left-handed, simply do the reverse.

FINDING YOUR GRIP

Hold your racket in your right hand, as if you are shaking hands with it.
Look at the "V" between your thumb and first finger (*see below*).
Make sure that this is at the top of the handle.

Look at the base of your racket's handle. You will see that it has eight sides. The "V" between your thumb and first finger moves around the handle, depending on the grip.

Use the "V" to help you find the correct grip.

FOREHAND GRIPS

There are four main forehand grips used for playing balls that are approaching you on your racket side.

EASTERN
This is a natural-feeling grip that is suitable for beginners. Simply hold the racket with the "V" of your hand on edge 2.

CONTINENTAL
This is a more advanced grip, which many players use for serving. The "V" should be on edge 1. The continental grip gives more power on certain shots. It also aids flexibility in the wrist and adds variety to your shots.

WESTERN
This grip started on hard courts, which produce high-bouncing balls. The "V" is positioned on edge 4. This grip feels awkward at first, because your wrist is wrapped right around the handle.

SEMI-WESTERN
The semi-western grip is a less severe version of the western. It is also used to hit high balls. The "V" is positioned on edge 3.

BACKHAND GRIPS

When a ball is approaching you on your left side, you will need to hit a backhand stroke. To do this, you can hold your racket with one hand or two. Most beginners choose the two-handed version, because it is easier to control. Try both grips, and use whichever one feels most natural.

ONE-HANDED BACKHAND

The most common one-handed grip is the eastern backhand. Rotate your wrist counterclockwise around the handle so that your "V" is on edge 8. To produce more topspin (see page 17) place the "V" on number 7.

TWO-HANDED BACKHAND GRIPS

right hand

left hand

You can use two grips when doing a two-handed backhand. The first is where you keep an eastern forehand grip with your right hand and add your left hand for power. The second is where your right hand changes from a forehand grip to a backhand grip, which keeps most of the power in your right arm—your left hand just helps support the racket. See which one feels the most comfortable for you.

WITHOUT CHANGE

Your right-hand "V" should be on edge 2 and your left hand should be on the handle, above your right hand, with its "V" on position 6 or 7, depending on comfort. The closer your left hand is to position 6, the more topspin (see page 17) you will be able to get.

WITH CHANGE

Rotate your right hand counterclockwise around the handle so that the "V" is on edge 8. Your left hand is above it, with the "V" on edge 7 or 6 (6 gives you more topspin).

TOPSPIN ONE-HANDED

This grips helps put topspin on the ball. Your right-hand "V" should be on edge 7. Your left hand supports the racket at the throat just until you swing the racket to hit the ball.

CHANGING YOUR GRIP

After playing a shot, come back to the ready position with the racket in front of you. At this point, you can change your grip according to your opponent's shot. You may find that you only need to use one or two of these grips throughout a match.

RULES OF PLAY

Tennis can be played as a singles—one player against another—or a doubles two against two match. The object of the game is to win points against your opponent. These points are scored to make games and sets. The winner is the first player to win either two sets in a three-set match, or three in a five-set match.

SERVING

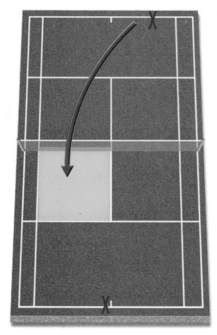

Once you decide who serves first, the ball is played diagonally into the service box opposite.

The server stands behind the baseline on the right-hand side. If the ball does not land in the service box, the umpire calls "second service" and the player has another chance. If the second service is not successful, then a double fault is called, and the opponent wins a point. If the ball hits the net cord but still lands inside the service box, then "let" is called and the service can be taken again. A let can happen on both first and second serves. After the first point is played, the server moves to the left-hand side of the baseline and serves diagonally into the other service box. The serves switch from left to right for each point. If a ball that has been served strikes the opponent anywhere before it has bounced—even if it was going out—the point goes to the server.

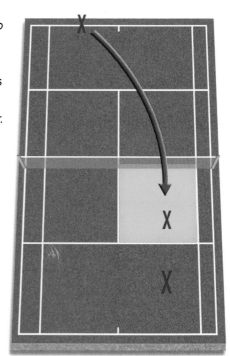

RECEIVING

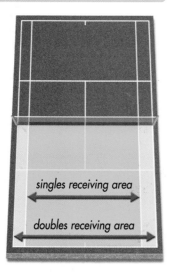

singles receiving area

doubles receiving area

If the serve is in the service box, the opponent returns it over the net to continue play.

The ball must land within the boundaries of the court. A point is scored by the last player to hit the ball over the net and into his or her opponent's side of the court. If the ball hits the net cord as it goes over, then play continues. The ball is only allowed to bounce once each time. In wheelchair tennis it is allowed to bounce twice.

CHANGING ENDS

Once the first game is won, the players change ends, and the service changes hands.
Afterward, the players change ends every odd (1, 3, 5, 7, 9) game, but service changes hands at the end of every game.

SCORING

Scoring in tennis has its own language and sequence.
For the first point in a game, a player scores 15, followed by 30 and then 40. If a player has no points then his or her score is called "love". For example, if the server wins a point, then the score is 15/love, because the server's score is always called first. To win a game, a player must win four points before his or her opponent wins three. If both players reach 40, "deuce" is called. After deuce, the score goes "advantage X" (X being the player who wins the next point) and that player must also win the following point to win the game. If he or she loses the point, the score goes back to deuce.

To win a set, a player must win six games before his or her opponent.
A player needs to win at least two games more than his or her opponent to win a set. If the players reach 5-5, then one player can still win the next two games to win 7-5. If they reach 6-6, the set goes to a tiebreak. In some tournaments, the deciding set cannot go to a tiebreak—the players must continue until one player wins by two clear games, i.e. 7-5, 9-7, 13-11, etc.

TIEBREAK

The object of the tiebreak is to be the first to score seven points.
One player serves the first point. After that, the service changes after every two points. If the score reaches 6-6, the first player to gain a clear two–point advantage wins the set, i.e. 8-6, 10-8, 12-10, etc.

DOUBLES

The rules for doubles matches are exactly the same, except that the doubles sidelines form the boundary of the court. The team players take turns serving and receiving from game to game.

WARMING UP

As you pound up and down the court during a game of tennis, you are working literally hundreds of muscles and tendons in your body. To protect them from injury and to maximize your flexibility, begin every match with a proper warmup and stretching routine.

FREE HIT

Before a match, you get a five-minute free hit to get a feel for the ball. Usually, players help each other warm up during the free hit. They use this time to practice forehands and backhands. They also take turns coming to the net for a minute or so to practice volleys and smashes. Keep relaxed—save your strongest shots for the match!

FITNESS DRILLS

Because tennis is a game of quick stops and starts, it helps to practice rapid, short bursts of movement. These drills improve speed and coordination.

FOOTWORK SQUARE

Stand in the bottom corner of the service box. Run along the center line to the net. At the net, stop and sidestep along it to the sideline. Now run backwards until you reach the service line. Finally, sidestep back to your starting position. Stay facing the net at all times. Do this cycle five times as fast as possible. Between each cycle, take a break that is about three times as long as it took you to finish the cycle.

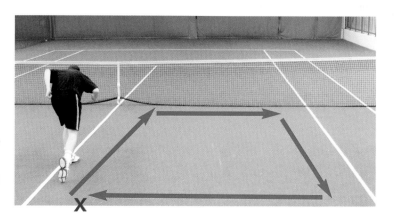

PICK-UP FITNESS DRILL

Crouch down behind the doubles sideline looking across the court, with four balls on the ground beside you. Pick up the first ball and place it on the first singles sideline ahead of you, then return, pick up another ball and run to the center line to place it there. Return for the third ball and run to place it on the far singles sideline. Finally, grab the fourth ball and place it on the far doubles sideline. Go back to the starting point and repeat the drill in reverse order. Again, take a break in between that is three times the length of the drill.

Begin your warmup with a gentle five-minute jog around the court—this warms and loosens the muscles. Start stretching, and take it gently. Never hold a stretch if it hurts—just take it to the point where you feel tension, and hold it for 10 or 15 seconds. Do not bounce when stretching.

ANKLE STRETCH

Lift each foot in turn so that only the toes are touching the ground. Gently turn your heel in both directions.

HAMSTRING STRETCH

Step forward with one leg and push the other out behind you to stretch the hamstring in the back of your leg. Repeat with the other leg.

INNER THIGH STRETCH

With one leg bent, extend the other sideways until you can feel the tension in your groin. Hold the stretch for 15 seconds and repeat with the other leg.

PELICAN STRETCH

Stand on one leg and gather your foot in your hand. Gently pull it back behind you. Stretch the muscle at the front of your leg by easing your toes toward your buttocks. Repeat with the other leg.

WRIST & ARM STRETCH

Extend your arms out in front of you. Cup one hand into the other and push your thumbs against each other to stretch your arms and wrists.

FOREHAND STROKES

*T*he forehand is the most common shot in tennis. It is often most players' best shot as well. The forehand is played when the ball is on your strongest side—your racket side—which gives you more control of the ball. The forehand can be aimed deep or wide into the opposing court. This shot is difficult to return. It puts your opponent under pressure and keeps him or her on the defence.

FOREHAND

The forehand is a groundstroke, which means that the ball is played after it has bounced.

STEP 1 From the split –step position, pivot your feet to the right to turn the shoulder. Begin to take the racket back.

STEP 2 Focusing on the ball at all times, bring your racket right back behind your shoulder. Stretch your other hand out for balance in the direction that you want the ball to go.

STEP 3 Step forward and swing the racket smoothly but firmly into contact with the ball.

STEP 4 Follow through with your racket reaching the opposite shoulder. Your body has now rotated naturally so that you are facing down the court. Notice how your weight has moved to your front foot, with the back heel now off the ground.

Topspin is the name for the spin that you put on the ball when you hit it in a certain way. Brush up underneath the ball instead of hitting it through the middle. When you hit the ball with topspin, it rises higher than normal over the net and bounces higher than normal when it lands. Pros use topspin often to confuse their opponents. This is a difficult technique to master, but it is worth the practice.

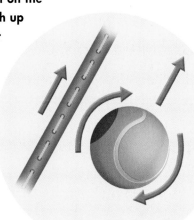

Bend your knees so that your body is low. As you make contact with the ball, brush your racket upwards on it, causing it to spin as you hit it. Your body should rise up with the ball.

OPEN–STANCE FOREHAND

The open-stance forehand is used to deal with higher-bouncing balls. It can be used with all forehand grips.

STEP 1 *Step across to the ball and bring your racket back.*

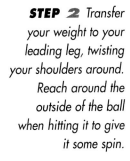

STEP 2 *Transfer your weight to your leading leg, twisting your shoulders around. Reach around the outside of the ball when hitting it to give it some spin.*

TOP TIP
Use the forearm to roll the racket around the ball a bit like a windshield–wiper action. This gives the ball more spin to stop it from going out of the court.

BACKHAND STROKES

When the ball comes to your non-racket side, you must bring the racket across your body and hit the ball with the other side. This shot is called a "backhand", and it can be played with either one hand or two.

TWO–HANDED BACKHAND

Approximately half of all players use a two–handed backhand. It has more power and control than the one–handed version has.

STEP 1
From the split–step position, turn and pivot your feet to the left. Bring your racket back and twist your body around so that your shoulder is square to the ball.

STEP 2
Bring your front foot forward so that you are facing the ball from the side.

STEP 3
In one fluid movement, swing the racket toward the ball. Your body should follow through naturally. Keep your arms loose and your grip firm as you bring the racket around to make contact with the ball, just in front of your body.

STEP 4
Continue to follow through with your racket, turning your shoulders and bringing your back foot around so that you face the net. You are now ready for the next shot.

TOP TIP
Try to vary your spins to keep your opponent guessing.

ONE-HANDED BACKHAND

The one-handed backhand is used to reach wider shots, although it may not give you the power of the two-handed backhand at first.

STEP 1
From the split-step position, turn and pivot to the left, so that your front shoulder is square to the ball. At the same time, bring your racket back across your chest, using your non-racket hand to grip the throat of the racket.

STEP 2
Step forward into the ball with your leading foot. Bend your knees and crouch down slightly as you prepare to make your swing.

STEP 3
Release the racket from your non-racket hand and smoothly swing it toward the ball. Face the ball from the side as you make contact with it in front of your body.

STEP 4
Follow through with your racket. Keep your elbow straight with your racket facing skyward.

SLICED BACKHAND

The sliced backhand keeps the ball low by putting backspin on it.

STEP 1
Using a continental grip, position yourself slightly wide of the ball and open up the racket face.

STEP 2
Slice the ball from high to low, and follow through with the racket parallel to your body. The ball bounces low to fool your opponent.

ON THE COURT: GROUNDSTROKES

*G*roundstrokes are shots where the ball bounces once before it is struck. Usually these are the forehand and backhand strokes. These drills are designed to help you practice proper placement. Placement is the skill of getting the ball to areas of the court that your opponent finds difficult to reach.

THROWN-BALL DRILL

This develops control of the ball and accuracy.

Pairs of players stand opposite each other in one half of a court. Player A from each pair throws a ball underarm so that it bounces in front of his partner, Player B, who is standing on the baseline. Player B plays a controlled forehand back for Player A to catch. After ten hits, the drill is repeated to the backhand.

PROGRESSION

Later, player A moves to the other side of the net. Using a racket, A hits the ball to player B, who has to play the groundstroke over the net. After each drill, player A gradually moves back until A plays the final drill from the opposite baseline.

TARGET SHOOTING

Target shooting improves accuracy to the areas of the court that are difficult to reach.

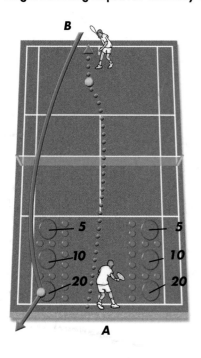

One half of a court is marked out with short colored cones indicating three target areas (see diagram). Player A feeds either a forehand or a backhand to Player B on the opposite baseline. Player B must aim a groundstroke to land it in one of the target areas. B scores either 5, 10, or 20 points as shown. Five points are taken away for any shot that lands outside any of the target areas. After 25 shots, the players swap roles. The winner is the one with the most points.

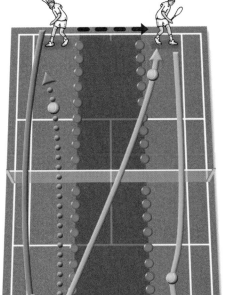

This drill develops accuracy in a rally situation.

A court is divided into three sections with cones (see diagram). Two players must then play a rally in which the central section is out of bounds. The players try to keep the ball in play within the legal areas.

This requires quick reactions and speed to keep the ball in play.

Player A feeds a ball underarm down the sideline to Player B's forehand. Player B returns it, crosscourt, to Player A's opposite corner. Player A runs across the court to play the ball down the line to Player B's backhand. Player B returns the ball, crosscourt, to where the drill began. After five minutes, the players swap roles.

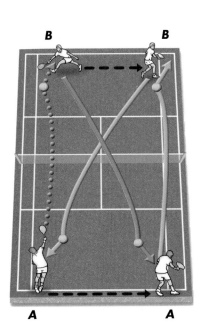

THE SERVE

The serve is probably the most important shot in tennis. It is also one of the most challenging. Having an excellent serve is a great advantage. A fast serve that lands close to the center or sidelines of the service box is always difficult to return.

HOLDING THE BALL

As you prepare to toss the ball, hold it lightly. The momentum of the ball will come from the upward swing of your arm, so you should simply release it. Do not flick it up with your fingers or wrist.

SERVING

Think of your serve as one continuous, fluid movement. When you're learning, don't try to hit the ball too hard. Focus on using a smooth, direct stroke.

STEP 1

Get your feet into position behind the baseline, with your side to the net. When you are balanced and ready, hold your racket out in front of you with the ball at the throat or against the strings.

STEP 2

Bring your hands down together and shift your weight from your front foot to your back foot, making sure that you focus on the ball.

STEP 3

Now bring your arms up together. Toss the ball up into the air, slightly in front of you. At the same time, your racket moves back into position, ready to hit the ball.

STEP 4

Watch the ball as it rises, bending your knees and shifting your weight onto your front foot. Bend your racket arm so that you bring your racket back behind your head.

STEP 5

As the ball reaches its highest point, straighten your legs and push up onto your toes. Stretch your arm for balance and drop the racket behind your shoulder, keeping your elbow up.

STEP 6

As you extend your racket arm, your shoulders rotate so that your chest faces the net as you hit the ball. Strike the ball at the highest point that you can reach. Bring your non-hitting arm back into your body as your racket goes forward.

Do not serve until you are ready. Bounce the ball a little to focus your mind, and take a deep breath to relax yourself before serving. If anything distracts your concentration, stop and start again.

STEP 7

Keeping your head up, follow the ball through, allowing your forward momentum to continue. Return to the ready position.

FOOT FAULT

Although you are allowed to jump into the court as you serve, your feet must not touch the ground inside the court or the baseline until the ball has been struck. If this happens it is called a "foot fault", and it will disqualify your serve.

ON THE COURT: THE SERVE

You get two chances to get the ball into the service area, but you always want to have a strong first serve. Nearly all players have a weaker second serve because they are nervous about double faulting and losing the point.

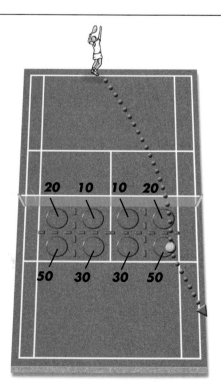

THROWING DRILL

Place a racket on the ground in front of your feet, pointing ahead of you. Then go through the motions of serving. Throw the ball so that it lands on the racket face every time. This will really improve your ball toss.

CONSECUTIVE SERVING

Practicing your serve often ensures more accurate service during a game.

One player serves to the other. If successful, he or she moves to the other side of the court to serve again. There are no second serves in this drill, so as soon as one player misses, the other takes over. Aim to serve 10 consecutive successful serves.

SERVING FOR DEPTH

This will enable you to practice and improve hitting deep serves.

Divide the service areas on one side of a court in half widthwise (see diagram). Two players serve two balls in a row, taking turns. The players score points according to where their serves land. After five minutes, the player with the most points wins.

20   10   10   20

50   30   30   50

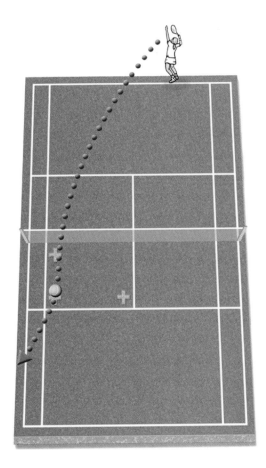

Once you have mastered getting the ball into the service area, you can try this drill to hit specific areas of the service box.

Place cones on the corners of one service box (see diagram). These are the three areas from where a serve is the hardest to return. A successful serve that is not returned is called an "ace". The aim of the drill is to hit the cones and knock them over. Players have 30 balls each and score ten points every time they hit a marker. The winner is the player with the most points.

This drill improves first–serve success in match situations.

Two players play a match, but with no second serves allowed. Now getting a successful first serve is even more important to the match than usual! This drill gets players used to serving under pressure—as they are on a break point.

SERVICE RETURNS

The kind of service return that you hit depends on the serve that you receive. Service returns are 50 percent of the game, and it is important to practice them as much as your serve. You will be a stronger player if your returns are just as tough as your serves are.

RETURNING THE BALL

Returning a serve is all about seeing the ball early and reacting to it quickly. Stand back from the baseline. It is always better to come toward a ball than to run backward.

STEP 1 *Stand in the ready position, roughly one foot (0.3 m) back from where you expect to hit the ball.*

STEP 2 *As your opponent tosses the ball, take a step forward.*

STEP 3 *Split step (see page 8) as your opponent strikes the ball.*

STEP 4 *As the ball leaves your opponent's racket, judge its flight and adjust your position to give yourself room. Turn to the side on which the ball is coming, and take your racket back. In this case, it is a forehand stroke.*

STEP 5 *As the ball comes toward you, step forward and bring your racket onto it. Make contact just in front of your body. Follow through with the racket and the power of your arm stroke. Keep your wrists firm, and use your non-hitting arm for balance.*

When the serve is very powerful, the best return is often a blocked–forehand return. The skill here is to hold the racket firmly, and angle it to punch the ball back over the net. The action is similar to a volley (see pages 30–31).

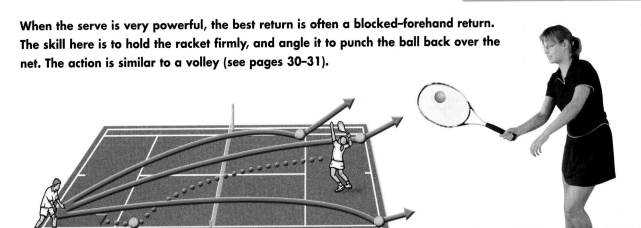

BACKHAND RETURN

STEP 1 *From the split–step position, turn your body to the backhand side. Quickly judge how much backswing you will need from the power of the serve.*

STEP 2 *Step forward to the ball. Watch it make contact with the racket as you keep your wrists firmly locked. Follow through to complete the return.*

ONE–HANDED BACKHAND RETURN

The same footwork rules apply to the one–handed backhand return. However, because you have a longer reach than with a two–handed return, this is a very useful return for reaching wide, sliced serves that are curving away from you.

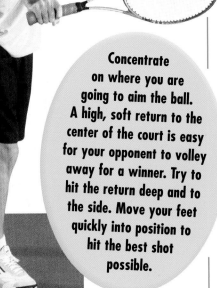

Concentrate on where you are going to aim the ball. A high, soft return to the center of the court is easy for your opponent to volley away for a winner. Try to hit the return deep and to the side. Move your feet quickly into position to hit the best shot possible.

ON THE COURT: SERVICE RETURNS

*O*nce you know the basics of groundstrokes, you can concentrate on adding power and direction to your return. Experiment with the grips to see which ones give you more control on certain serves.

BASIC RETURNS

Start with easy shots to build up your service–return confidence.

Player A stands just behind the baseline of the court. Player B hits a medium–speed serve over the net and into the service box for Player A to return. Practice for ten minutes, and then swap places.

PROGRESSION

Once both players are hitting the ball cleanly and getting it back over the net regularly, start trying to place your shots close to the sidelines and the baseline.

FAST RETURNS

Returning a hard and fast serve is all about reading the serve and getting into position quickly.

Player A stands just behind the baseline, while Player B serves from the service line on the other side of the net. However, this time Player B plays a full speed serve into the service box. Player A must attempt to return these hard, fast serves.

ATTACKING RETURNS

Use this drill to practice playing accurate and aggressive service returns.

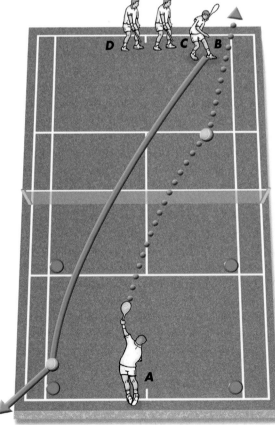

Place cones at one end of the court (see diagram). Player A stands at the same end as the markers and serves. Player B must try to hit one of the markers with his or her return. Every hit scores 10 points. After five minutes, Player B goes to the back of the line. Player C repeats the drill, followed by Player D.

The cones represent the perfect points to aim for when hitting a return of serve. Your opponent will have to run to get the ball, giving him or her less time to make a successful shot.

TOP TIP
Take smaller backswings to block big, fast serves.

THE VOLLEY

Avolley is a shot that is played before the ball has bounced, usually from an attacking position close to the net. You are not swinging when you play a volley. Instead you simply redirect the ball, using the angle of the racket head to send the ball back over the net.

FOREHAND VOLLEY

You can volley a ball using any of the forehand grips. However, a continental grip is good for reaching the angle of a low volley.

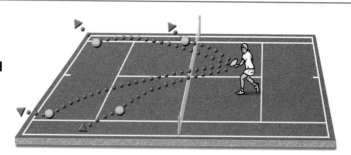

STEP 1 *Get yourself into position about 5 feet (1.5 m) from the net, and stand in the ready position. Split step as the ball is played, and prepare to receive the shot.*

STEP 3 *Step forward with the foot on your non-racket side, shifting your weight onto the front foot as you position your racket to meet the ball. Angle the racket to direct the ball toward one of the sidelines or away from your opponent. Do not follow through after contact.*

STEP 2 *With the ball coming toward you, turn and pivot your feet in the direction of the ball. Keep your racket ahead of you and angle it in the direction of the ball. Pull your racket back very slightly.*

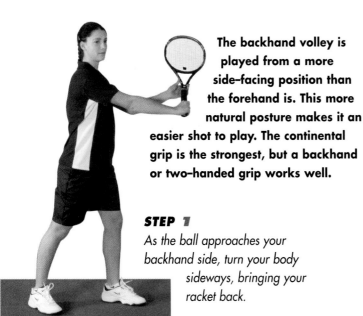

The backhand volley is played from a more side–facing position than the forehand is. This more natural posture makes it an easier shot to play. The continental grip is the strongest, but a backhand or two–handed grip works well.

STEP 1

As the ball approaches your backhand side, turn your body sideways, bringing your racket back.

BACKHAND VOLLEY

STEP 2

Step forward to meet the ball, then bring the racket under the ball to angle it back over the net. Keep the wrists locked and the racket up. Following through slightly after contact will give more punch to the stroke.

HIGH–FOREHAND VOLLEY

To reach a high ball, bring your shoulders around slightly so that you can reach up and over the ball to punch it down. Hold the racket after you have made contact to avoid sweeping the ball down into the net.

HIGH–BACKHAND VOLLEY

This stroke requires good timing. Play it sideways, stretch out your free arm for balance, and squeeze the grip as you make contact with the ball. You can use your other hand for extra support or put your thumb up the back of the grip.

LOW–FOREHAND VOLLEY

Lunge forward with the front foot on your non-racket side, and bend your knees to get your body low. Keep your head up, and tilt your racket face to get it under the ball. The momentum from the ball will lift it back over the net. Keep your back as straight as you can, keeping the racket head above the wrist at all times.

LOW–BACKHAND VOLLEY

Approach the ball from the side, and step forward with the front foot on your racket side. Bend your knees and go down to hit the ball. Hold your body position, and freeze your racket for a split second. This will give you the right amount of power to make the volley. Keep the racket head above the wrist.

ON THE COURT: THE VOLLEY

Hitting a controlled volley takes plenty of practice, and these drills are designed to slowly build up your skills at the net. A well–hit volley is almost impossible to return and is a lethal weapon in a player's armory.

THE "NO RACKET" VOLLEY

This teaches you the basic footwork and body position required to hit a good volley.

Two players, without rackets, stand opposite each other, about 12 feet (4 m) apart. Player A throws a ball in the air to player B's forehand side. Player B must step forward with the opposite foot and catch the ball just in front of him with his racket hand. Player B then repeats the exercise for Player A. After practicing the forehand side, the players should switch to a backhand catch.

VOLLEY DEVELOPMENT

This drill slowly builds you up to hitting technically correct volleys.

STEP 1
Two players stand on opposite sides of the net, 12 feet (4 m) apart. Player A throws the ball to Player B's forehand side. Player B, holding the racket at the throat, must volley it back. This is much easier than hitting a volley holding the racket by its handle.

STEP 2
Standing in the same position, Player A throws the ball for Player B to volley it gently back, this time holding the racket in the normal position.

STEP 3
Finally, Players A and B both use their rackets and volley the ball between each other.

VOLLEY PAIRS

The previous drills concentrated on volleying on the spot. Use this drill to volley while on the move.

Players get into pairs and line up on one side of the net. The first pair begin volleying the ball to each other. At the same time, they move across the court, parallel to the net. They are followed by the second, and then the third pair. Each pair must not let the ball bounce or hit the net until they reach the other side. Repeat the drill using a variety of forehand and backhand volleys.

AT THE NET

Use this drill to practice defensive volleying at the net against hard, attempted passing shots.

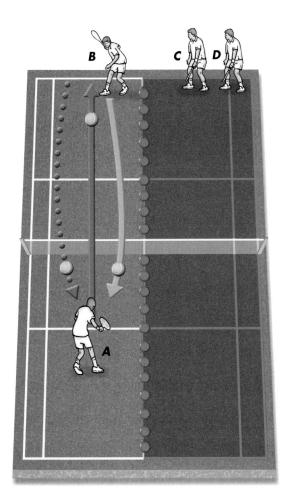

Using marker cones, the court is split down the middle on both sides of the net (see diagram). Using only one half of the court, Player A starts from the service line and feeds underarm passes to Player B on the baseline. Both players then rally, with Player A on the service line and Player B on the baseline. Player A must volley on every shot. After the rally, Player B goes to the back of the line, and Player C repeats the drill, followed by Player D.

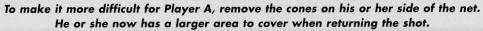

TOP TIP
To make it more difficult for Player A, remove the cones on his or her side of the net. He or she now has a larger area to cover when returning the shot.

THE LOB

*T*he lob is a shot that is played high into the air and over an opponent who has come toward the net. It is an excellent stroke, because it can force an opponent to play the return from a difficult angle and weaken his or her position in a rally.

FOREHAND LOB

It is important to hit this ball correctly. Too hard, and it will go out of bounds, but too soft, and you will present an easy smash (see pages 38–39) to your opponent. This stroke is often performed with an open, or upturned, racket, but a closed one gives the ball topspin and makes it harder to return.

STEP 1 As the ball bounces, keep your legs apart, and bend your knees as you get your racket back early.

STEP 2 After the ball has reached the top of its bounce, rotate your shoulders back, and bring your racket around underneath it. Now lift the ball into the air.

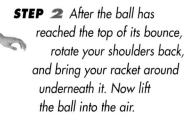

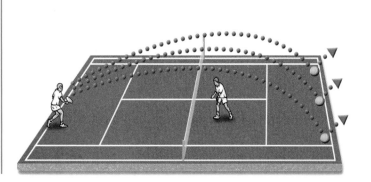

STEP 3 Straighten your legs as you follow through, making sure that you don't underhit the ball. Aim to lift the ball over your opponent's racket, while keeping it within the bounds of the court.

ONE-HANDED BACKHAND LOB

Power from the lob comes from the shoulder. You can play this shot with either an open racket face or a closed racket face for more topspin. It is more of an attacking shot if it is played with topspin.

STEP 1 *Turn sideways to the ball, and bend your knees as you take your racket back to a point below where you will hit the ball.*

STEP 2 *When the ball begins to fall after it has bounced, sweep your racket underneath to hit it.*

STEP 3 *Use your non-racket arm for balance as you straighten your legs. Rotate your shoulders back toward the net, and follow through with the shot.*

TWO-HANDED BACKHAND LOB

If you can put topspin on the ball when you lob it, you can give it more height, and it will bounce sharply away from your opponent. In this case, your non-racket hand gives you more control.

STEP 1 *Turn your shoulders back and drop the racket below the wrist.*

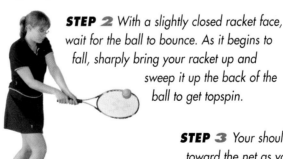

STEP 2 *With a slightly closed racket face, wait for the ball to bounce. As it begins to fall, sharply bring your racket up and sweep it up the back of the ball to get topspin.*

STEP 3 *Your shoulders turn toward the net as you follow through. Straighten your legs, and rotate your back leg up onto your toes.*

TOP TIP
If your lob forces your opponent to run back to retrieve the ball, move to the net to attack the return with a volley or smash.

ON THE COURT: THE LOB

The lob is one of the hardest strokes to master. It requires the player to hit the ball high into the air without it landing outside the court. These drills enable you to perfect the action of lobbing the ball up above your opponent's head to land in the court.

DEEP LOBBING

Use this drill to practice hitting lobs as far back into your opponent's court as possible.

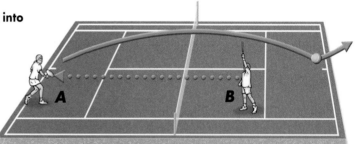

Player A stands on the service line and feeds balls to Player B on the opposite baseline. Immediately after the feed, Player A raises the racket above his or her head. Player B must return the ball by lobbing it over Player A to land in the back section of the court.

TOP TIP

Try to lob onto the opponent's backhand side. This will cause the player to hit a difficult backhand smash. Now you are in a good position to win the point.

TARGET LOBBING

Since the lob is such a difficult shot, use this drill to help you gain better control and direction over it.

Divide the end of a court into four boxes, and allocate points for each section (see diagram). Player A stands in the center of the service line and feeds balls to Player B at the opposite baseline. Player B must lob the balls back over Player A's head, aiming for the scoring boxes. Add the points up each time the ball lands in one of the boxes. After 20 shots, the players swap roles. The winner is the one with the most points.

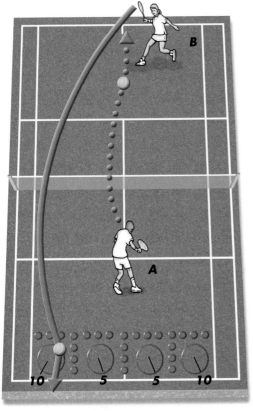

THE SMASH

The smash is an attacking shot that is played when the ball is in the air above your head. You need to play it with confidence. A weak smash can be returned with a shot that forces you to run backwards to reach it. Running backwards always weakens your position in the rally. On the other hand, a strong smash is a sure way to win a point.

FOREHAND SMASH

You can use an eastern grip to get instant results when you are learning. Change to a continental grip as you gain confidence. This grip gives the shot more power and spin.

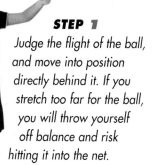

STEP 1
Judge the flight of the ball, and move into position directly behind it. If you stretch too far for the ball, you will throw yourself off balance and risk hitting it into the net.

STEP 2
Watching the ball, bring your racket back behind your head as far as it will go and turn sideways. Use your non-racket arm for balance and as a guide for the direction of the ball.

STEP 3
Throw the racket head at the ball as it comes down, and aim to hit the ball at its highest point. Angle your racket to hit the top of the ball so that it will clear the net.

STEP 4
Follow through so that your racket ends up around your waist. This slows your body down and lets you get into position for a possible return.

The backhand smash is one of the hardest strokes to play. You have to twist your racket around behind your back, then bring it over your shoulder to smash the ball.

STEP 1

Turn your body and feet to meet the ball sideways. Support the racket with your free hand as you take it back. Your elbow should be pointing in the direction that you want the ball to go.

STEP 2

Release the racket, bringing it up over your shoulder to make contact with the ball. Hit the ball, angling your racket so that it clears the net. Put your body weight behind the shot for added power.

STEP 3

Follow through, using your free arm for balance, then get back to the ready position.

TOP TIP

Try to imagine hitting the ball over a high wall when smashing it. This will help you reach up for it before the ball drops.

ON THE COURT: THE SMASH

When you get a chance to smash in a match, it is important to kill the point then and there. If the shot is returned, use your whole body to get maximum power behind it, making it as hard as possible to return a second time.

THE "NO HIT" SMASH

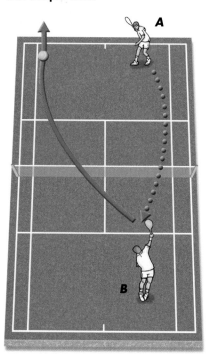

The smash requires excellent balance and footwork. Use this drill to learn to anticipate the movement of the ball in the air.

Two players stand opposite each other on either side of the net. Player A throws the ball into the air above Player B's head. Player B gets into position facing sideways, with his or her racket back and his or her non-hitting arm fully extended above him or her. As the ball comes over, he or she should catch it to become familiar with the flight of the ball.

SMASH TO OPEN COURT

Build up confidence in your stroke using this simple drill.

A

B

Player A stands at one end of the baseline and feeds a high ball to Player B, who is standing in midcourt. Player B must smash the ball back into the open court. To add a competitive edge, each player has 20 smash attempts, scoring one point for every winning shot and five points for hitting a line.

ANGLED SMASHING

Practice smashing the ball to the corners of the court.

Using cones, mark out four boxes at one end of the court (see diagram). Player A stands at this end of the court and lobs balls to player B on the other side of the net. Player B smashes the ball back, aiming for the target boxes. After 20 shots, the players swap roles. The winner is the one with the most points.

PROGRESSION

In a match, you are often running back when you hit a smash, because your opponent is trying to lob over you. To recreate this situation, Player B should run forward and touch the net between each shot.

THE DROP SHOT

A drop shot happens when you hit the ball so that it drops over the net with a soft bounce. This shot draws a player out of position by forcing him or her to come in to the net. If your opponent is caught deep behind the baseline, a surprise drop shot can be next to impossible to return.

FOREHAND DROP SHOT

You can play the drop shot when you are close to the net, using your preferred forehand grip. The eastern grip is used in this demonstration.

STEP 1

As the ball approaches you, take your racket back farther than you would for a volley. Step forward onto your non-racket foot.

STEP 2

Once the ball reaches you, slice the ball as it is rising with a slight downward motion of the racket. Reduce your follow–through as if playing a volley. This shot is performed by applying a firm grip but having "soft hands", or a light touch.

TOP TIP
Take your racket back early to disguise your drop shot. Your opponent will think that you are about to hit a normal groundstroke and not expect the gentle drop.

BACKHAND DROP SHOT

This can be played with one or two hands. Use your preferred backhand grip.

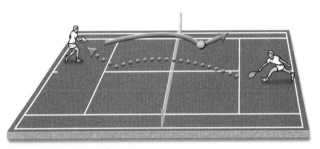

STEP 1

Face sideways to the ball and pull your racket back.

STEP 2

As you step forward, reduce your swing and slice the back of the ball as it rises. Keep your follow–through short. This shot should be played with a slightly open racket face at contact.

DROP VOLLEY

This is a drop shot that is played before the ball has touched the ground.

Approach this shot in the same way that you would approach a normal volley, but angle your racket up more. As you make contact, loosen your grip so that the racket head moves back slightly and the strings absorb the speed of the ball. The ball should just drop neatly over the net. Use a forehand or backhand stroke, depending on the direction of the ball.

DIET

Y ou can give yourself more energy and stamina on the court by eating and drinking the right foods both before and during the game. A healthy diet and regular exercise are good for anyone, but these things are essential to become a top athlete.

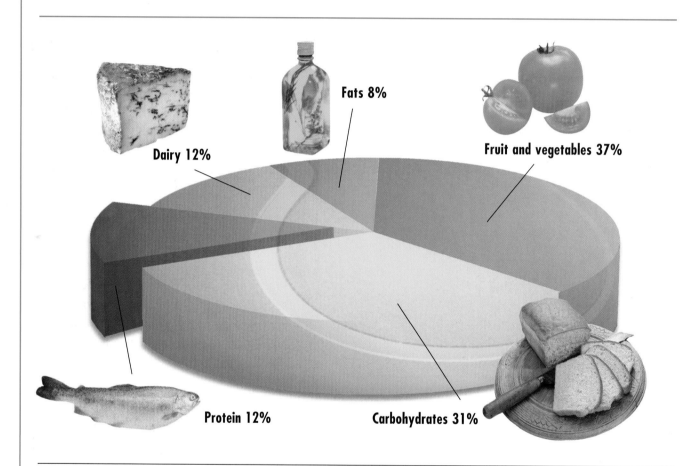

Dairy 12%

Fats 8%

Fruit and vegetables 37%

Protein 12%

Carbohydrates 31%

FIGHTING FIT

Tennis is a grueling, non-stop game, so you should choose your food according to your match schedule. Try not to eat too much before a game.

A light, balanced meal about an hour and a half before a match is best.

A tennis match can last from one to four hours. Be sure to have lots of fluids before, during, and after a match. Water is the best drink, although the body needs some sugars. Add a small amount of fruit juice to the water, or use a sports drink. It is very important to stay hydrated at all times.

ENERGY BOOSTERS

Carry fast-digesting snacks, such as bananas or fruit-snack bars, to keep your energy levels up— especially if the game is a long one.

Do not eat sugary foods. This will give you a quick burst of energy but then leave you feeling tired.

MENTAL ATTITUDE

It is important to prepare the mind as well as the body for a tennis match. The best skills in the world are worth little if you do not believe in yourself. Self-confidence is as necessary as a great serve to a tennis player.

VISUALIZE SUCCESS

During a game, take some time alone to focus your mind on the task ahead.

Use positive thinking and concentration to visualize yourself winning the next point, the set, and the match. If things are going badly or a decision goes against you, control your temper. You must learn not to get upset or lose confidence.

FIT FOR THE TOP

All professional tennis players do other activities to enhance their performance.

Golf is perhaps the most preferred second sport for tennis players. It allows them to relax and be active without risking injury.

MIND OVER MATTER

There is nothing like winning a game to give you confidence.

An outward display of joy after winning a hard-fought game can put pressure on your opponent. Tennis is as much a battle of wills as one of technical skill.

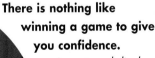

HOW THE PROS DO IT

Most people play tennis for fun. The very best players in the world are professionals who travel the world playing the game AND get paid for it. However, don't think it's all glamour in the world of a tennis pro. It takes hard work and dedication to make it to the top...and even more work to stay there.

TYPICAL MATCH DAY

8.00	Wake up
8.30	Eat a low-fat, high-energy breakfast with no fried foods
9.00	Arrive at the event venue
9.15	Warm up/stretch
9.30	Practice on court with a coach or another pro
11.30	Eat a light lunch
12.00	Discuss prematch tactics with the coach
12.30	Rest and stretch/change into uniform
2.00	Play a match
4.00	Attend a postmatch press conference
4.30	Do a light gym workout/stretch
6.00	Swim/massage
7.00	Return to the hotel
8.00	Eat a high-carbohydrate dinner
9.00	Watch a video of the match with the coach
10.30	Go to bed

LIFE ON TOUR

Professional tennis is played by men on the ATP Tour (the Association of Tennis Professionals) and by women on the WTA Tour (the Women's Tennis Association).

The top four grand-slam events are the Australian Open, the French Open, Wimbledon, and the U.S. Open. Other events occur from Austria to Saudi Arabia—this means that most players are always flying around the world as they compete to pick up crucial world-ranking points. Roger Federer won three of the four Grand Slam titles in 2004 and 2006.

The major tournaments offer large prizes for first and second place. However, many players in the top 100 ranking can have a great career in tennis.

Serena and Venus Williams, seen here, won the women's doubles final at Wimbledon in 2000. Prize money varies with each tournament, but the winner of the mens singles final can receive in excess of $1,000,000!

MONEY

For the top players, the rewards in tennis can be enormous.

Stars like Maria Sharapova can earn millions from sponsorship deals with companies such as Nike, who want these athletes to promote their products. However, it is generally only the top-seeded players who secure such profitable deals.

THE PRESS & MULTIMEDIA

Doing TV and radio interviews is all part of the daily routine for successful tennis players.

Win or lose, after a match, they are expected to attend a press conference to talk about the game. On top of that, they will be asked to do exclusive interviews and photo shoots with TV stations and publications. Many players and associations have their own web sites that are updated regularly—particularly during a major tournament.

GLOSSARY

ADVANTAGE – *An advantage is given to a player when he or she scores a point after deuce.*

ACE – *A serve that lands within the court boundaries without being returned.*

BACKSPIN – *When the ball is struck at the bottom by the racket, causing reverse spin.*

BACKSWING – *When the racket is taken back to hit the ball.*

BLOCK – *A shortened stroke that uses the momentum of the ball to carry it back over the net.*

CENTER MARK – *A mark on the baseline that indicates the serving position.*

CHOPPER GRIP – *Another name for the continental grip.*

CROSSCOURT – *The action of going diagonally across the court.*

DEUCE – *When the score in a game is 40/40.*

DOUBLE FAULT – *When both serves fail to land in the service box.*

DRIVE – *A term used to describe a forehand or backhand groundstroke.*

FAULT – *Any action in tennis that goes against the rules.*

FLIGHT – *The path in which the ball is traveling.*

FOLLOW–THROUGH – *The natural path that the racket takes after it has hit the ball.*

HALF VOLLEY – *A volley that is played just as the ball hits the ground.*

LET – *When a serve hits the net but lands in the service box.*

LOVE – *The tennis equivalent to zero.*

MATCH POINT – *The point that decides the winner of the match.*

NET CORD – *A ball that hits the net as it goes over. It is only called a let when this occurs during service.*

POINT – *What is scored at the end of a rally or single shot.*

PASS – *A shot that goes over an opponent at the net.*

RALLY – *A series of shots played back and forth between players in order to win a point.*

RECEIVER – *A player who is waiting to return a ball.*

RETURN – *A shot that is played back over the net from the previous shot or serve.*

SIDESPIN – *The spin created when the racket hits the ball from left to right or right to left, causing it to bounce sideways.*

SET – *When a player has won six games or beaten the opponent by two clear games.*

SECOND SERVE – *A serve that is taken when the first one has been deemed a fault.*

SLICE – *The racket action that puts backspin or sidespin on a ball.*

SPLIT STEP – *A small bounce that is made just before playing a shot.*

TOPSPIN – *The forward rotation of the ball that causes it to bounce high on landing.*

TRAMLINES – *The parallel lines of the singles and doubles sidelines.*

UNDERSPIN – *When the ball is struck at the bottom, causing reverse spin.*

VOLLEY – *A shot played before the ball has the chance to bounce.*

WESTERN – *An exaggerated style of grip that produces topspin.*

INDEX

Printed in the USA